CRYPTOCURRENCY REMOTE VIEWED

BOOK ONE

KIWI JOE

THE KIWI JOE SHOW

Watch now on YouTube!

Don't forget to like and subscribe.

ALSO IN THE REMOTE VIEWED SERIES

Cryptocurrency Remote Viewed : The Top Twelve

Cryptocurrency Remote Viewed : Book Seven

Cryptocurrency Remote Viewed : Book Six

Cryptocurrency Remote Viewed : Book Five

Cryptocurrency Remote Viewed : Book Four

Cryptocurrency Remote Viewed : Book Three

Cryptocurrency Remote Viewed : Book Two

Cryptocurrency Remote Viewed: Book One

Book One (eBook only) is *FREE* to download!

Most Secret Weapons of Nations Remote Viewed

Fukushima Radiation Solution Remote Viewed : Engineering an End to the Radioactive Leak

Forrest Fenn's Treasure Remote Viewed : The Location

Forrest Fenn's Treasure Remote Viewed : The Chest

ISBN-13: 978-0-6485680-4-9

CONTENTS

INTRODUCTION

Did you know that you can unlock the secrets of a cryptocurrency's future through the lens of remote viewing?

Better than that, you can use remote viewing to predict the future of individual cryptocurrency projects. In this book I examine six of them, each drawn from a blind pool of cryptocurrency projects I assembled on the 28th of October, 2020. These were the top 200 coins and tokens as listed on online ranking sites, such as CoinMarket-Cap.com on the date shown at the start of my analysis for each of the coins I cover.

My goal is to remote view one hundred coins and tokens. Whether or not I actually cover that many crypto targets will depend on the response of readers, and sessions that continue to deliver consistently good information. I have tested the search question I use to collect the remote viewing data for this cryptocurrency series many times and it continues to deliver satisfactory results. We refer to the initiating search question of our remote viewing session as a **Cue**.[1]

Please note, the insights I provide in this book are intended to complement authoritative cryptocurrency information from more conventional sources. For instance, one such source is a project's White Paper, or WP.[2] We refer to the information collected during a remote viewing session as **Data**. This is the kind of information most cryptocurrency enthusiasts, investors, and blockchain developers will not have access to, and, for the most part remain unaware of. It is the kind of information that makes remote viewing such a great tool for research.

By the way, I am a remote viewer. I am not a financial advisor and nothing of what follows is to be considered financial advice. The information I give you is intended as a guide to help your research and for those readers who are simply interested in cryptocurrency or remote viewing.

Remote viewing data can be compared to the cold, logical insight an insider can provide combined with the subjective understanding of someone recalling a past event. There isn't much that can be hidden from a seasoned remote viewer. While that may seem a bold claim to make, it was the potential of controlled and applied ESP—an ability natural to humans—to be an effective tool to use to spy on foreign militaries that led to the development of this skill in the first place. The fact that remote viewing produces statistically significant results is a good part of the reason secretive government departments around the world have spent so much money on developing the skill, and I think it likely continues to this day.

To ensure the validity of the data, I remain blind to the target throughout a remote viewing session until after I sign off on the final page when I view the cue to see how I fared. A crypto target is randomly selected from a large pool of possible cryptocurrencies. There are some two hundred targets in the blind pool. All I see when I start a remote viewing session is the randomly generated line of numbers assigned to the target. This approach limits bias and foreknowledge that might otherwise corrupt my data.

I delve deeper into this method in Chapter Three. The chapter is aimed at readers who may not be remote viewers, but who may be knowledgeable about the cryptocurrency targeted or perhaps about blockchain technology in general. It does get more complex than this, but we need not go that deep in this series. Suffice to say here, the cryptocurrency pool I have put together is large enough to effectively blind me to the **Target**.[3]

I use the same cue throughout the cryptocurrency

series. While the target changes, the search question asked does not. The target is automatically deleted from the pool once it appears in a session, ruling out the possibility the same cryptocurrency is targeted more than once. I use software to enable the process whereby I select a target from the blind pool.

Traders may find that they aren't the primary audience, but the remote viewing data can still be of value to them too. A coin that's going to be an ultimate winner will likely show its form along the way to its destination. There are three reasons why I did not have traders in mind when I wrote the cryptocurrency series.

First, remote viewing effectively targets objects, concepts, even thoughts, but the timing of a future event adds a whole other level of complexity. While collecting data on whether or not a particular coin or token will be successful is fairly straightforward, trying to nail down the year, month, or day that it reaches its highest or lowest value is a different story.

In short, attempting to uncover a temporal aspect means accepting a level of uncertainty I am not happy dealing with in this series. It isn't so much that this is an impossible task, it is just that it is far more difficult to consistently get right. The ideal approach would be to have a team of remote viewers on the job. I am the only remote viewer collecting the data for these books. This is the reason I include a chapter showing readers not trained in remote viewing how to do the analysis of the raw data. I will say more about this below.

The second reason is that a remote viewer working the same target over and over again can quickly reach saturation point. They must take a long break from the target type, or they risk going batshit crazy. Okay, there are politer ways to put that, but they lack the same emotional charge.

Collecting quality data becomes difficult if not impossible if the conscious analytical mind is allowed to intrude on the session. The risk associated with repeatedly remote viewing the same cryptocurrency for its peaks and plunges is of reaching the point I can no longer make sense of the target. I think it best I avoid the possibility of that happening altogether.

So long as readers express interest in the books, or until I have remote viewed one hundred cryptos, whichever happens first, I will continue with the series.

The third reason I did not have traders in mind when I started the series is the simplest. I happen to favor HODLING.[4] One question on the minds of most when they probe the value of a cryptocurrency is this. Does the cryptocurrency address a real-world problem? When I probe for information as a remote viewer, I look for strong indications the crypto project meets the objectives stated in its WP, or that it does not. If it does, then I expect to see it increase in value over time.

A successful crypto project will usually be one that fairly consistently introduces a few groundbreaking developments that cater to its market. If so then it is likely its popularity increases and as a result so does the funding it receives.

So, I'm not overly concerned about a crypto project's peaks and troughs as it makes its way toward ultimate success. In a nutshell, I assume long-term, a successful crypto project will meet its objectives as they are set out in the WP. This is how I am measuring the success of a crypto project.

As far as the remote viewing data is concerned, I settle for clear indicators the ultimate future of the cryptocurrency is that it's considered a success. By 'ultimate future' I mean the cryptocurrency's long-term success as seen in the rearview mirror, so to speak. I want to see data showing the project is alive and kicking and stirring public interest right up until it finally succumbs to the inevitable just as everything must one day. I also hope the data I collect points to a future rise in value and the cryptocurrency's obvious success.

About my role as the data collector: a remote viewer must record the information as they collect it without altering any of it. To this end, I follow an exacting protocol that scaffolds me through a series of steps designed to eliminate the conscious mind from the process. It is the discipline imposed by the protocol and the training required that separates a remote viewer from a psychic.

A psychic may gain insight via a vision, a dream state, chanting, a flash of premonition, or simple intuition, but remote viewing shares more commonalities with a witch doctor who examines chicken bones thrown in the dust, or an ancient aunty who insists on reading your tea leaves every time you visit. However, that is where the likeness ends. The discipline imposed by following a remote viewing protocol allows more consistently accurate information than most witch doctors or great-aunts can muster.

I don't necessarily pinpoint the reasons behind a coin or token's success or failure. I expect that the cause will be evident in the data, but this may not be clear because the cue I use is not focused on looking at a cause. To do so requires more remote viewing. However, often enough indicators show up in the data. A limited knowledge of blockchain technology doesn't help me recognize everything the data presents to me. My strongest remote viewing skill is definitely collecting the data.

Those of you with a background in blockchain technology, or who have spent time researching it, will have a distinct advantage over me when it comes to analyzing the raw data. For that reason alone, I urge you to do your own analysis, and in this book and throughout the series, I provide you with the tools to do just that.

Know there will always be the possibility a crypto project fails, no matter how deserving it may be in terms of its stated objectives. A project may become redundant if the solution they provide no longer matters to the market or the cryptocurrency loses out to a more agile competitor. Consider the outcome of the videotape format battle for market supremacy that waged between Betamax and VHS in the late 1970s. The best team doesn't always win. If we lived in a fair and just world they would, but unfortunately, we don't.

I'd very much like to believe all my sessions are accurate, but I must be realistic, and so, I aim for a success rate of around seventy percent or better. In other words, I allow thirty percent of the sessions will prove incorrect in the long term. This is the 'Kiwi Joe had a bad day' factor that inevitably weighs in no matter how careful I am during the remote viewing session or how well prepared I was for it beforehand.

I recommend readers supplement their research with my data. You can improve the odds in your favor by looking at what the more traditional experts have to say about the cryptocurrencies I cover. Readers also may want to compare my conclusions to those of other remote viewers whenever possible.

In the back of the book you can find a bibliography of remote viewing titles. While far from comprehensive, the list of books is a good place to start if you are interested in learning more about this learned skill that utilizes the phenomenal natural ability we all have to some degree.

Please note, this book is intended as a free sample of the series. The discussions on the cryptocurrency project's background and the analysis of the remote viewing data are kept fairly brief. I cover those areas in much more depth in the books that follow. Stay tuned for more remote viewing insights on various cryptocurrencies. Keep an eye out for new releases in this series.

If you enjoy this book please consider leaving an honest review or a quick rating. A line or two from you will make all the difference to another reader's decision. And, I really appreciate your support.

---

1. A cue is designed to gather data specific to the target. I discuss this in more detail in Chapter Three.

   NB: All the key remote viewing terms used in this book are introduced in bold type.
2. The White Paper is an informative and authoritative report or guide that sets out the key features of the technology, the real-world problem it addresses, and the solution it was created to provide.
3. The term 'target' in remote viewing can be versatile. Often, when we mention 'targeting', we use it as a verb. We also use the word as a noun, which is to say we are using it to name something. For

example, we talk about a particular target site. We will also talk about Aspect X as being the target aspect in a site template sketch.

I talk more about this in Chapter Three. The chapter is aimed at readers who may not be remote viewers, but who may be knowledgeable about the cryptocurrency targeted or perhaps about blockchain technology in general. It gets more complex, but we need not go that deep for this series.

4. Legend has it the term HODL began as a misspelling of 'hold' on an online forum called Reddit. Whatever its origins, HODL is widely considered an acronym of 'Hold On for Dear Life' as in 'to continue to hold the cryptocurrency no matter how bad the volatility'.

CHAPTER ONE

IN THE VAST *world of cryptocurrency, two key players stand out: coins and tokens.*

A coin operates on its own unique blockchain and primarily serves as a medium of exchange. Digital coins function in other ways too; for instance, the coin DASH gives users voting rights. Bitcoin (BTC) is without question the best-known of all the cryptocurrency coins.

Several cryptocurrencies have 'coin' in their name, but are technically tokens. For example, Binance Coin (BNB) is technically a token. While a coin can stand alone, a token can't. Similar to phrases like 'token gesture' or 'token gift', a cryptocurrency token represents something else.

First, a blockchain is established, followed by the

creation of a token for its use. Generally, tokens offer broader functionality than do coins. Many tokens allow access to a decentralized application known as a dApp. One example is the Basic Attention Token, often referred to as BAT, which is built for use on the Brave Browser.

After a token is created, the next step is often coin creation. The transition from a token to a coin typically occurs via a 'coin swap' or 'token swap' process. VeChain (VET) is an example of a project having completed the swap process. Once the testing phase concludes and the new blockchain is ready, a coin replaces the token. As you might expect, the process is more complex than this brief overview suggests. For a deeper dive into this intricate topic, consider exploring dedicated books on the subject.

An Initial Coin Offering (ICO) is the cryptocurrency equivalent of an Initial Public Offering (IPO). However, when an investor puts money into a company releasing an app, service, or actual coin, they are not buying shares. In return for their investment, they receive a token, not the actual coin. Investors purchase the token hoping the ICO project will take off and the value increase. Often, raising funds involves releasing a whitepaper (WP) as part of a marketing campaign.

Funding an ICO project does not necessitate an already established blockchain. Since tokens are easier to create than coins, they are typically issued first. The release of a token or coin does not guarantee its success. Some projects will keep going for some time yet fail to become the success story they marketed themselves to be. Many ultimately fizzle out.

Cryptocurrency projects may fail for many reasons. Reasons might include a competitor boasting a superior programming team, having more funds to navigate the volatile early stages, leveraging a groundbreaking technological advancement—possibly from their own team—or simply outperforming others by efficiently addressing real-world problems. The failure of a crypto project is likely due to a combination of these and other factors.

Note: Throughout this series, I use the word 'coin' when talking more generally about cryptocurrencies. For specific projects, I differentiate between 'coin' and 'token' based on blockchain affiliation.

CHAPTER 2
READING THE DATA WITH EASE

IN THIS CHAPTER, *I give you the necessary tools to unearth the mysteries of crypto using the power of remote viewing.*

Before jumping straight into the six crypto projects I cover in this book, let's familiarize ourselves with a few key concepts and terms. These are important to understand in order to reveal relationships between the different parts of the target. These can be easily missed or even hidden. You can, if you prefer, leave all the analysis to me. I have included a summary list of my conclusions in Chapter Ten.

Remote viewing gathers information without the viewer being physically present at the target site nor having any prior knowledge of it. For those unfamiliar with remote viewing, it involves a strict protocol that ensures data collection is objective and free from distractions. To this end, we follow a rigid protocol: collecting and recording data using a structured method. This approach minimizes the subjective comments and imaginings that could corrupt our results.

The protocol also ensures that the data is recorded as efficiently and objectively as possible. The time to complete a remote viewing session is strictly limited, so there is little opportunity for the remote viewer to be distracted. To further limit the possibility of mistakes and to optimize results, a remote viewer usually works the session alone and always in a room free of distractions. Admittedly, that's a fairly dry introduction, but let's delve into the more intriguing aspects of this learned skill.

In a remote viewing session, our unconscious mind interprets data according to our perceptions that have been shaped, for the most part, by our life experiences. For example, the interests and knowledge of a nuclear physicist might overlap with what catches the eye of a nuclear engineer, but both specialists may still miss features obvious to a trawler captain, a software developer, a clothes designer, and so on. Eventually, we all become specialized in one field or another, and it is this experience that frames the way we see the world.

When it comes to analyzing cryptocurrencies, my life

experience may not serve me quite as well as your first-hand knowledge of blockchain technology, coding, or more general information technology. If you think you recognize what I might miss in the data, then go with that thought and do your own analysis using the tools I give you in this chapter.

The run-through of how to apply the tools should be enough to help you interpret the sketches. There are two in each of the six chapters. I regard this raw data as my most significant contribution in the book and the larger series.

The Cue

By default, the cue focuses only on the data needed. It filters out anything that would confuse the search. Much like a specific search in a comprehensive library, a cue is crafted to yield helpful answers. One of the key elements in learning to remote view is knowing how to construct a precise search question that defines the data.

To ensure the results are reliable, a new remote viewing cue is tested before it is used in a session. No matter how skilled a remote viewer might be, if they do not ask the right question, the answer they get back will be worse than useless. Because the remote viewing cue is so specific, all data recorded that is not eliminated by following the protocol during a session must be considered relevant to the inquiry. Learning how to cue properly is a skill that takes time and practice to master. Cues can be proprietary, and those most prized are handed down from teacher to trusted student.

Being Blind to the Target

A remote viewer is usually blind to the target when they work a session, but not always. The remote viewing session begins with a unique sequence of randomly generated numbers (or a mix of numbers and letters) linked to the hidden cue. This sequence of digits is called a '**Target Reference Number**' (**TRN**). It functions as a key that allows the remote viewer access to data. Since the remote viewer usually has no idea of the cue until they finish the session, they are effectively blindfolded as they collect and record data. This helps ensure the data is reliable.

A remote viewer works their session completely blind to the target. All they see at the start is the number sequence. The TRN can be located in the top left-hand corner of an ST sketch. If you are a remote viewer you might want to use the TRN to run your own session on the coin.

The Matrix

A remote viewer considers the data to come from the **Matrix**, and no, this has nothing to do with the movie series starring Keanu Reeves. Imagine the matrix as a vast decentralized library that surrounds us, encompassing everything we're aware of and more. It contains all the information that's ever existed and will ever exist.

This concept is equivalent to the proverbial *ether*, but be aware that it has nothing to do with mysticism or magic. Rather remote viewers see the matrix as explainable in terms of our material world, to put it another way, the skill that is remote viewing targets reality, be that lifeform, inanimate object, concept, or even the thoughts of others. Unfortunately, traditional science as taught in the academy struggles with the reality of remote viewing.

When we tap into the matrix, we do so via the **Signal Line.** Science has not yet conclusively demonstrated the existence of the signal line, so it remains a theoretical concept just like the matrix. As Lyn Buchanan, the well-known remote viewer dryly puts it, remote viewers use such terms to "look semi-intelligent" when what they are really saying is "I don't know where the information comes from".[1] If you are interested in finding out more about these fundamental concepts informing what we know as remote viewers, do take a look through the titles in the reference list at the back of this book.

The important thing to understand about the matrix at this point is that it doesn't care if the information it reveals is officially available for the public to see or not. Yes, remote viewers really do tend to think of the matrix as an all-knowing entity rather than as a dry concept. There is always the possibility those standing behind a particular cryptocurrency project may prefer the public don't recognize the information revealed to the remote viewer. Keep in mind, the matrix shows only data relevant to the cue. It's up to the remote viewer to capture the data and record all of it transparently. The data may reveal critical aspects of the project that even the developers and team leaders are not aware of.

Remote viewers quickly learn that when it comes to data, it simply is what it is. Remote viewing deals with the truth, no matter how unpalatable it may turn out to be. The bottom line is we must treat all our data as being important.

Analytical Sketches

To analyze means to describe and explain. In this case, we are describing and explaining the data assembled in the two sketches you will find in the cryptocurrency chapters. First, put together an ST sketch. The follow-up sketch is called an S6. You may be disappointed by the minimalistic appearance of the analytic sketches. A good part of the reason for this is the time constraint imposed by the remote viewing protocol. This time limit allows for only simple line drawings to be rendered.

The ST page takes the longest time of any to complete. There is only so much detail you can include in a short time frame. Of course, this also means everything you see in the sketches is relevant to the analysis that follows.

There are preliminary sketches that lead up to the ST. It is not necessary I say more about these here, but only to mention they are quickly sketched. For this reason, we favor the use of archetypes over detailed features. Archetypes here refer to the basic representation of an object. Archetypes are basic symbols used to depict objects, like using an upside-down V to represent a mountain. In practice, remote viewers may provide more detailed elaborations on these archetypes. It depends on the amount of contact they have with the signal line during the session, but this really is a case of less-is-best. Some archetypes to be aware of in this book are as follows.

- *Right angles* indicate man-made structures.
- *Arrows* indicate a vector. For our purpose, a vector simply means a directional force. My apologies to those

physics folks who will be disappointed that mine doesn't include magnitude. Vectors indicate directional movements, like those of water or air currents. In this book, they usually show the direction of light or electrical energy. Usually, what the arrows represent is made clear by the nature of the aspects and the way they relate to one another in the ST.

- *Diagonal crosshatched lines* indicate a solid mass. These are not to be confused with perspective indicators —the larger crosshatched lines that fan out from the far horizon.[2]

The ST

Each cryptocurrency chapter showcases two distinct sketches. The first, known as the ST page, shows the significant features of the targeted cryptocurrency. The ST is the culmination of the base remote viewing session. It is also the most complex sketch.

The ST brings together the significant things described by the data. Remote viewers refer to these as **Aspects**. Each crypto project features just three key aspects. That's an artificial limit I impose to keep within the scope of the book series. The target aspect is called **Aspect X**. Because it may be made up of several elements on the page, I highlight it in color for easier identification.[3] The other two aspects are called **Aspect A** and **Aspect B**. While the ST may seem abstract, what you are looking at are the three key features of the targeted cryptocurrency.

In addition to sketches, the data also comes in text form. In the ST, all text data is in capital letters, consistent with the analysis that follows. I explain more about text data in the sensories section below.

The Future-Predicting S6

After completing the ST, a second sketch, the S6, is undertaken to allow for a deeper dive. The data I gather from the S6 consists of higher-level attributes, the nature of which depends on the type of inquiry. The focus of interest could be a specific aspect within the ST, or it could encompass the entire ST. A remote viewer, for instance, might use the S6 to probe into the past to determine the cause of an event. Alternatively, they could delve into the future to predict an outcome.

In the Cryptocurrency Remote Viewed series, I use the S6 to predict what lies in the ultimate future for the targeted cryptocurrency. Is it success or failure? We want to know about the most relevant future event. In the matrix, all future events are predestined.

I understand that this section was probably the most

difficult to digest for those readers here primarily for the cryptocurrency information. By comparison, the rest of the chapter is relatively straightforward.

Decoding Sensories: The Textual Data

This refers to text data associated with a particular aspect in the ST. In general, **Sensories** include things, concepts, and symbols. They can be single words or even phrases. These can be distinguished in a number of ways. I have chosen to present them in two groupings, words and phrases that are capitalized, and those that are not. As I previously pointed out, sensories that are capitalized in a sketch are also capitalized in the analysis that follows. The text data is considered equal in significance to the sketched aspects.

Also included in the analysis is text data that are not capitalized. This uncapitalized text data, which does not appear in the sketches, describes what the remote viewer experiences of the ST during the session. Although the remote viewer is not physically at a target site sensations are realized and recorded during the session as if they were. These are considered secondary sensories to the capitalized terms and phrases, but they are to be considered of equal value to the analysis.

These secondary sensories can be grouped into

various categories. Those I include in this series are as follows. There are colors, and other qualities of light, movement, sound, dimensions, positioning, and weight. Other types of secondary sensory appear within quote marks. They indicate whatever words or phrases the remote viewer might have overheard or seen during the session. For example, the company name seen on the side panel of a truck. Not all these types of sensories are recorded in every session.

Words or phrases that are preceded by a series of letters are remote viewing acronyms. Those appearing in the series are the following:

AI: The Remote Viewer's Emotion

The acronym **AI** in remote viewing work indicates the sensory attached is an emotion felt by the remote viewer. AI captures the viewer's emotional response during data collection. While an aspect might look relatively innocuous as sketched and as most of the text data present it, if the remote viewer's experience of it was distinctly unpleasant they will have indicated as much by recording the exact kind of emotion as an AI. A second emotion type may also be recorded in the ST. It should not be confused with an AI.

• • •

EI: Target Site Associated Emotion

An EI indicates the emotion felt by at least one lifeform. An EI in the ST indicates the presence of a lifeform, even if a living thing is not depicted in the sketch. In summary, while an AI reflects the remote viewer's emotions, an EI depicts the emotions of lifeforms at the target site. By default, an EI records the presence of a lifeform at the site, or if not physically present, their association with it. An AI should not be confused with an EI.

AOL/S: Tapping into the Signal Line

Occasionally, you will see an AOL/S entered into an ST, related to what is known as an **AOL**. You won't see the latter in this book, but I do need to mention it at this point. An AOL is a recurring idea recorded during the session as an imagining. Remote viewers follow a procedure to eliminate it, ensuring data purity. Students are taught early in their training how to recognize AOLs and reject them outright. When they appear, they are regarded as the analytic mind attempting to make sense of the data by interpreting it as a remembered thing.

I mention AOLs for two reasons. Firstly, to reassure readers that remote viewers are aware of the threat posed by imagination. If the analytic mind intrudes unaddressed during a session, it can render the raw data nonsensical or distract viewers from recognizing genuine data from the matrix.

Secondly, although you won't find an AOL in the data I introduce the important concept to explain the AOL/S. When an AOL persists despite following clearance protocols, it can be identified as an AOL/S. The remote viewer treats the AOL/S as a clear indication they have established a strong connection with the signal line. The sensory, prefixed with the acronym AOL/S is then entered in the ST as significant data.

---

1. www.crviewer.com
2. I use crosshatching to suggest perspective when I think the position and size are of significance. This technique is used in design and architecture to good effect and doesn't seem to conflict with the remote viewing protocol.
3. Color graphics only apply to the eBook copies. Please check your device can show color if the STs appear in black and white.

   At present, the ST pages in paperback copies are printed in black and white. I would much rather they be seen in color as in the ebooks. However, a color print necessitates a level of price increase to compensate for the increased printing cost I am not comfortable with. I look forward to increased sales to allow a color print.

CHAPTER 3
HOW WE DO THIS

EMBARKING *on a crypto journey with the power of remote viewing? Here's what you need to know.*

There are just a few more pointers to cover before we get to the remote viewing sessions and the cryptocurrencies. Each of the data and analysis chapters begin with a snapshot of the coin's status at the time of writing, intended to judge how well my data holds up in the future when the majority assess the crypto project's success or failure.

Each cryptocurrency is accompanied by a brief description, its official website, and a link to its WP. To discover the original objectives of the project you should refer to its WP.

About Spelling Mistakes and the Unconscious Mind

During remote viewing, it's common to encounter spelling mistakes due to the specific state of mind. Many remote viewers refer to this as 'the unconscious mind', which I equate to the mental discipline martial artists pursue. Remote viewing harnesses our innate psychic abilities. It's a disciplined skill acquired under an adept tutor. If you're intrigued, check the end of this book for my learning recommendations.

When remote viewers record raw data, in sketch or text form, they are capturing data they experience when working a session. If of the visual kind, these are most often experienced as vague forms rather than photo-like images. The abstract sketches you'll see in the upcoming chapters are the end result of the strict protocol remote viewers must follow, combined with the nature of remote viewing data. The point of following the remote viewing protocol is to collect unfiltered data from this state of mind as efficiently as possible. This should help explain the frequent spelling errors seen in remote viewing STs.

Since we are in an unconscious mind state during the capturing and recording, spelling mistakes are simply par for the course. It is later during the analysis stage, once we have completed the remote viewing session, that any spelling errors are realized. To underline this point, the analytical mind is the opposite of what I mean by 'the unconscious mind'.

I prefer to write these books using American English, but you may see the occasional British English expression in the data. Mistakes like a dropped letter may appear, and it's not uncommon to enter this kind of mistake on a page during a session as it is almost an inevitable consequence of employing the unconscious mind. Rest assured, I've corrected for such errors in the analysis.

Analyzing a Conceptual Target

Cryptocurrencies are intangible targets comparable to computer programs. Imagine buying a coffee with cryptocurrency from your phone. Such transactions are logged on a decentralized public ledger called the blockchain. This ledger, distributed across a network of computing devices like laptops, smartphones, even cars, makes the blockchain an elegant solution. All these devices must be online at some point to log a transaction.

While the invention of the blockchain solves many technological and real world problems, it remains complex computer code. This is what makes these targets largely conceptual. In the case of cryptocurrency, there are also associated material objects that might also show up in the data, adding to the degree of difficulty associated with remote viewing this type of target. These are tangible items, such as people, facilities, and countries.

Sometimes, a name associated with the cryptocurrency appears, other times it may be a face. See the S6 sketch in Chapter Five as a case in point. A face identifies a unique individual, and in analyzing such data, it's ideal to identify who they are. A face appearing in an S6 may relate to the reason for a cryptocurrency's success or failure. For reasons I won't delve into here, specific individuals associated with a targeted cryptocurrency project aren't typically expected in the data. Nevertheless, when they do appear, we take notice.

While we speak about the matrix as being the source of our remote viewing data, whatever data is recorded in the restricted time allowed by the protocol is whatever our unconscious mind finds most interesting at the target site. The unconscious mind of the remote viewer is the independent variable. The data the remote viewer collects during a remote viewing session reflects the nature of the target, but the way they interpret the target is influenced by their experiences, expertise, and background.

CHAPTER 4
VELAS (VLX)

ABOUT VELAS

Price in USD: $0.044288

Market Cap[1]*: $93,232,612*

Circulating Supply: 2,105,150,749 VLX (this amount is 100% of the total supply).

[Date and Source: 28 October, 2020; https://coinmarketcap.com/]

WP: https://velas.com/VELAS-Technical_Paper.pdf

Official Website: https://velas.com/

Background

Velas is a blockchain that uses proof of stake and is operated and delegated by artificial intelligence. According to the team, it's the first of its kind. Velas includes several efficiencies for smart contracts and decentralized apps created for use on it. It offers scalable transactions, reaching up to 30,000 per second. A wallet for Velas is available within the system.

Analysis

ST - Velas: The ST is shown below.

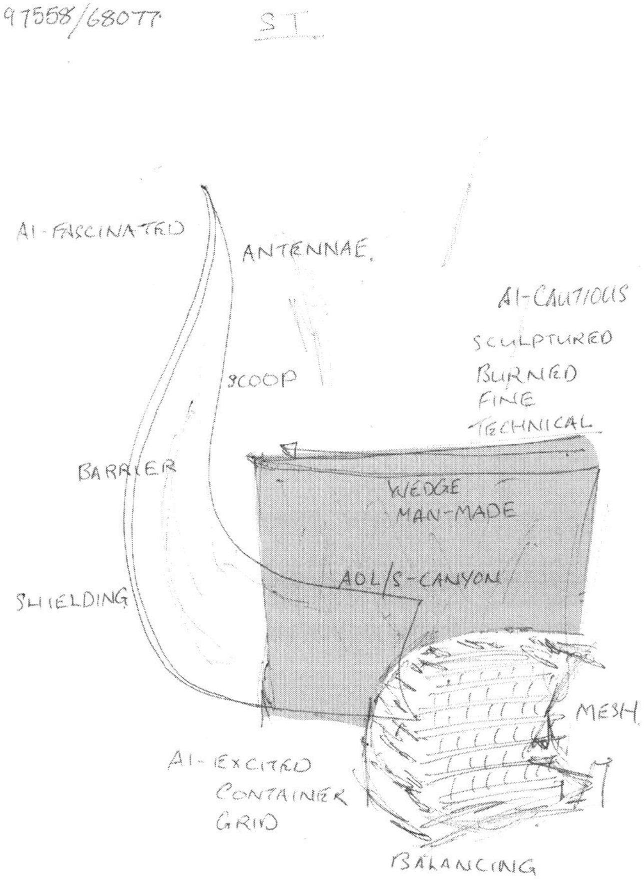

97558/68077
S I
AI-FASCINATED
ANTENNAE.
AI-CAUTIOUS
SCULPTURED
BURNED
FINE
TECHNICAL
SCOOP
BARRIER
WEDGE
MAN-MADE
AOL/S-CANYON
SHIELDING
MESH
AI-EXCITED
CONTAINER
GRID
BALANCING

Overview of the ST Sketch

The three target aspects are closely associated. Aspect X is the pink-colored man-made wedge positioned behind Aspects A and B. Aspect X is always considered the target aspect. I will color it in each ST.

Aspect A is most prominent. It's a scoop acting as a barrier. Aspect B is an open mesh in the form of a grid that sits in the foreground.

X

There's the strongly recurring idea of a CANYON.

Aspect X is a thick, pointed, huge, and deep WEDGE that is MAN-MADE. It is associated with SCULPTURED, BURNED, FINE, and TECHNICAL. There is movement from the fat end toward the pointed end. It is making an echoing sound.

It makes me feel CAUTIOUS.

A

Aspect A is a coppery red-colored, shiny, and metallic SCOOP that is a BARRIER. It is big and wide but also curved, tall, and thin. It makes whistling and clicking sounds. It is associated with ANTENNAE and SHIELDING.

It makes me feel FASCINATED.

. . .

B

Aspect B is a black-colored, small, thin, and open MESH that is a GRID. It is heavy. It is associated with CONTAINER and BALANCING.

It makes me feel EXCITED.

S6 - The Ultimate Future of Velas

The final page of data from the remote viewing session follows.

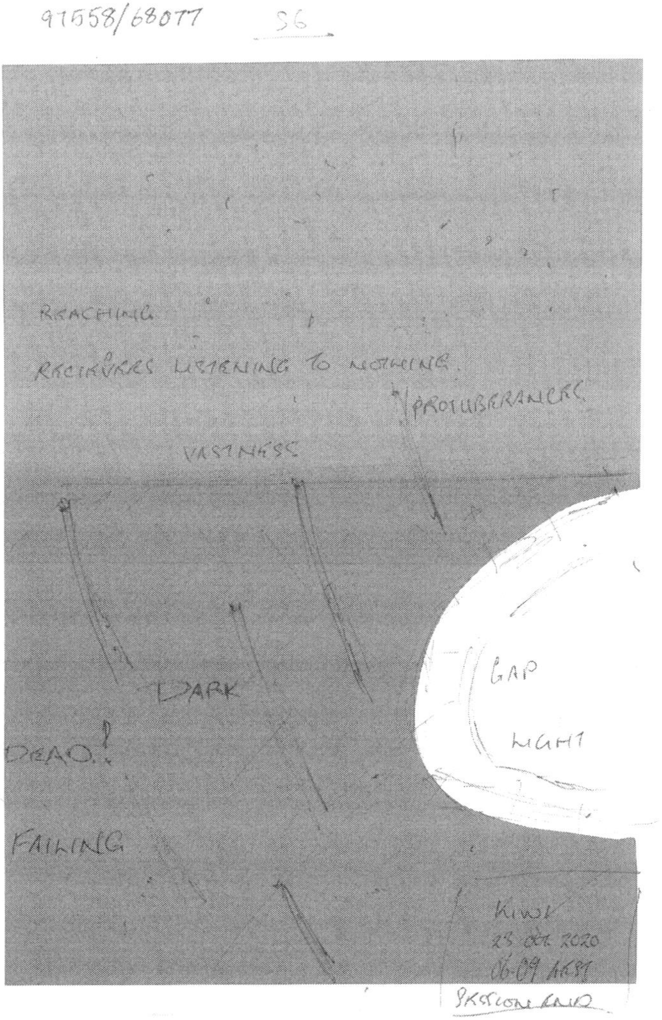
97558/68077
S6
REACHING
PROTUBERANCES
VASTNESS
DARK
DEAD?
FAILING
GAP
LIGHT
KIWI
23 OCT 2020

There's REACHING.
There are RECEIVERS LISTENING TO NOTHING.
There are PROTUBERANCES.
There is a VASTNESS.
There is DARK.
There is DEAD!
There is FAILING.
There's a GAP where there's LIGHT.

Comments on the S6

The most revealing data in the S6 are the first lines of text on the page, REACHING and RECEIVERS LISTENING TO NOTHING. These two lines indicate a project rendered redundant, perhaps for reasons beyond its control. In which case, the solution Velas offers would be no longer required. On the right side of the page, the presence of LIGHT highlights the dominance of the DARK underlined by DEAD and FAILING.

My Conclusion for Velas

The S6 data doesn't present a rosy future for Velas. It appears the project meets with an obstacle that proves to be insurmountable. Or perhaps Velas faces competition that not only surpasses but also eliminates the crypto.

While it is possible to identify the reasons the crypto fails, doing so requires more remote viewing, and that investigation falls outside the scope of this book and the series.

Keep in mind that thirty percent of these sessions may be inaccurate. If you're a supporter of Velas, consider my assessment with caution. Based solely on my S6 remote viewing data, my conclusion is that Velas might not be a solid investment.

---

1. The market cap is a standard metric in the cryptocurrency industry. It is calculated by taking the current market price of the cryptocurrency in question and multiplying that by the total number of coins in circulation.

CHAPTER 5
CHAINLINK (LINK)

ABOUT CHAINLINK

Price in USD: $12.10

Market Cap: $4,714,612,906

Circulating Supply: 389,509,556 LINK (38.95% of the total supply).

[Date and Source: 28 October, 2020; https://coinmarketcap.com/]

WP: https://whitepaperdatabase.com/chainlink-link-whitepaper/

Official Website: https://chain.link/

Background

Chainlink addresses smart contract connectivity issues. As a solution, it offers a "highly reliable decentralized oracle network" with security on par with the smart contracts.

Analysis

ST - Chainlink

The ST for this session follows.

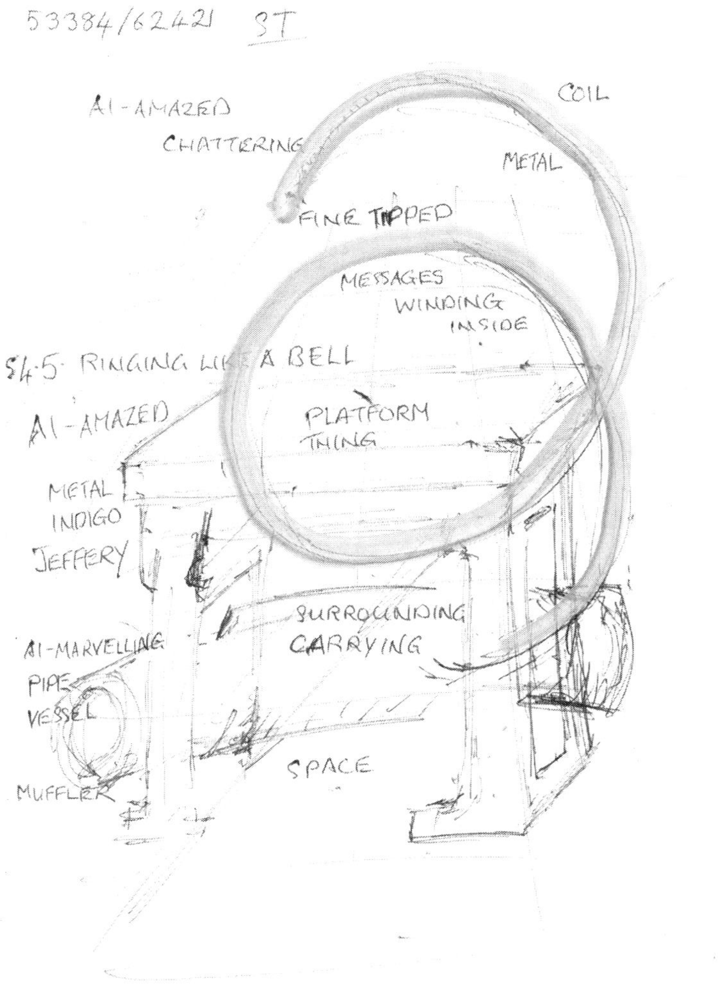
53384/62421 ST
AI-AMAZED
CHATTERING
COIL
METAL
FINE TIPPED
MESSAGES
WINDING
INSIDE
S4.5 RINGING LIKE A BELL
AI-AMAZED
PLATFORM
THING
METAL
INDIGO
JEFFERY
SURROUNDING
CARRYING
AI-MARVELLING
PIPE
VESSEL
MUFFLER
SPACE

Overview of the ST Sketch

The three aspects are closely associated. Aspect X is a metal coil. It is big, and positioned over the other aspects. Aspect A is a pipe under a structure that resembles a three-legged stool. Aspect B is a platform where the pipe rests (beneath its stool-like top).

X

Aspect X is a shiny, copper-colored COIL made of METAL. It is associated with CHATTERING, WINDING, MESSAGES, and INSIDE. It is big, curving, high, and positioned over something. There is the idea of FINE TIPPED.

It makes me feel AMAZED.

A

Aspect A is a long, thick, hollow, dark, curving PIPE that's positioned over something. It is associated with SURROUNDING, CARRYING, VESSEL, and MUFFLER.

I am MARVELING at it.

. . .

B

A shiny, reflective, and black-colored THING made of METAL is a high, straight, angular, dense, thin, open PLATFORM that's placed on something. It is associated with INDIGO, JEFFERY, and SPACE. There's the idea of RINGING LIKE A BELL.

Once more I feel AMAZED.

S6 - The Ultimate Future of Chainlink

The final page of data from the remote viewing session follows.

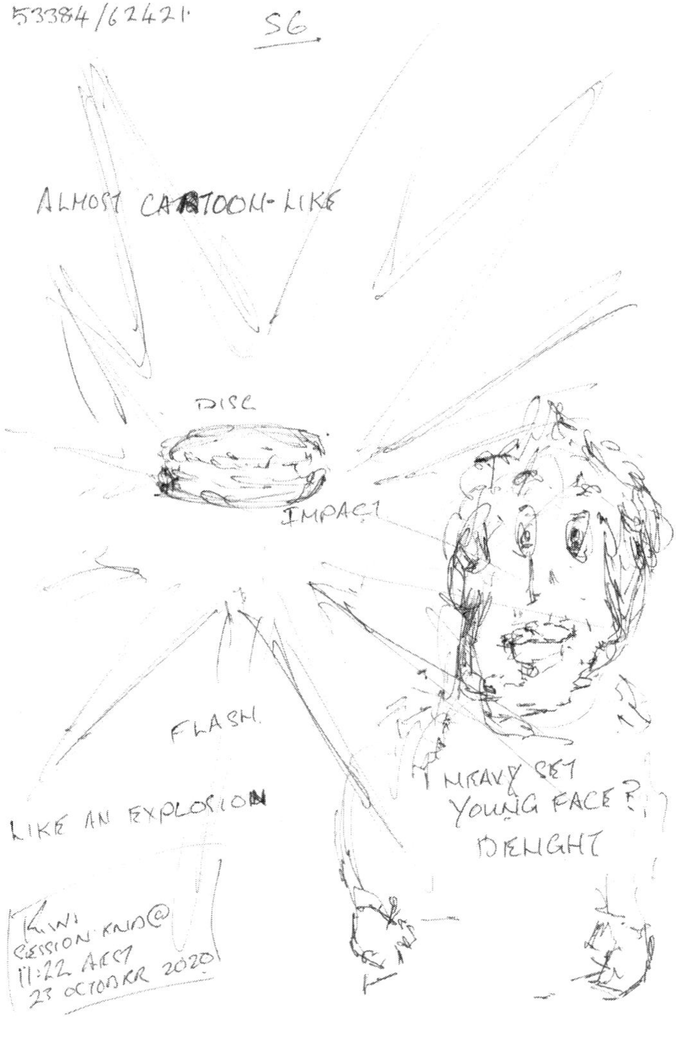

53384/62421
SG
ALMOST CARTOON-LIKE
DISC
IMPACT
FLASH
LIKE AN EXPLOSION
HEAVY SET
YOUNG FACE?
HEIGHT
KIWI
SESSION KNID@
11:22 AEST
23 OCTOBER 2020

It's ALMOST CARTOON-LIKE, with a central DISC-like object.

There is IMPACT.

There is a FLASH. It is LIKE AN EXPLOSION.

There's a HEAVY SET person with a YOUNG FACE.

There is DELIGHT.

Comments on the S6

The data suggests a stunning and rapid uptake for Chainlink. I see no indication this is a project that will fizzle out. The S6 data shows good things are in store for Chainlink.

So, who is the figure in the S6? The sketch shows the face of a blonde and wavy-haired, chubby man. He likes what he is seeing. The detail tells me this is someone significant. Perhaps he is a key developer or an investor in the crypto project. Could this be the "JEFFERY" mentioned in the ST data?

My Conclusion for Chainlink

In conclusion, based solely on the remote viewing, Chainlink is a crypto project worth further investigation. Its ultimate future looks good.

Based on the S6 data alone, I must say Chainlink looks to be a keeper.

CHAPTER 6
KUSAMA (KSM)

ABOUT KUSAMA

Price in USD: $33.95

Market Cap: $287,554,505

Circulating Supply: 8,470,098 KSM (87.76% of the total supply).

[Date and Source: 28 October, 2020; https://coinmarketcap.com/]

WP: https://guide.kusama.network/docs/en/kusama-index

Official Website: https://kusama.network/

Background

Kusama provides a development environment on a highly scalable network for projects aiming to "push the limits of what is possible." Relatively low cost is just one of the advantages offered to developers. In addition, the project encourages its own growth as well as that of the industry as a whole by bringing multiple blockchains together to test 'fast-moving' projects and foster rapid innovation from early to mid-development.

Analysis

ST - Kusama

The ST for this session follows.

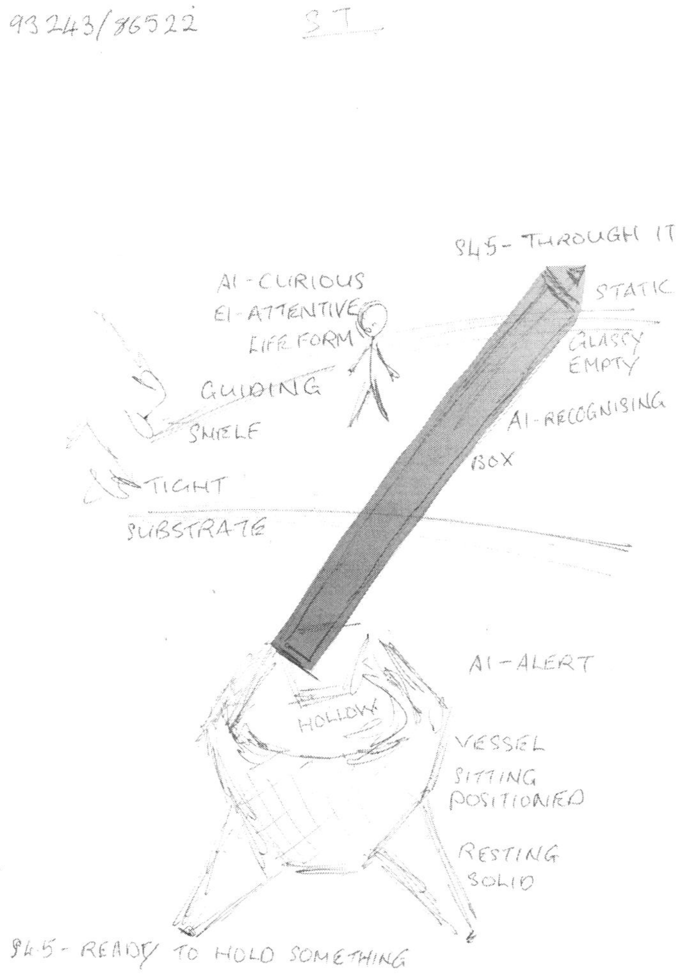
93243/86522
S T
94.5 - THROUGH IT
STATIC
AI - CURIOUS
EI - ATTENTIVE
LIFE FORM
GLASSY
EMPTY
GUIDING
AI - RECOGNISING
BOX
TIGHT
SUBSTRATE
AI - ALERT
HOLLOW
VESSEL
SITTING
POSITIONED
RESTING
SOLID
94.5 - READY TO HOLD SOMETHING

Overview of the ST Sketch

Aspect X is a long, rectangular-shaped, hollow, transparent BOX positioned on a diagonal. I've colored it purple.

Aspect A is a LIFEFORM, a person standing on a surface that forms a SHELF. They are at some distance from Aspect X and Aspect B. Aspect B is an open **HOLLOW VESSEL** that looks like a pot on two legs positioned in the S.T. below Aspect X (the long rectangular BOX).

X

Aspect X is a big, long, thin, hollow BOX illuminated in bright light and sitting on a diagonal above something. It is associated with STATIC, GLASSY, and EMPTY. There is energy traveling along the length of it in a northeast direction. There's the idea of going **THROUGH IT**.

I'm RECOGNIZING it.

A

Aspect A is a LIFEFORM standing on and over a curving, bright SHELF with something scattered below to one side of it. This person feels ATTENTIVE. They are associated with GUIDING, TIGHT, and SUBSTRATE.

It makes me CURIOUS.

B

Aspect B is a dark, curving, heavy, and HOLLOW open VESSEL that is on something. It is associated with SITTING, RESTING, POSITIONED, and SOLID. There is the idea it is READY TO HOLD SOMETHING.

It makes me feel ALERT.

S6 - The Ultimate Future of Kusama

The final page of data from the remote viewing session follows.

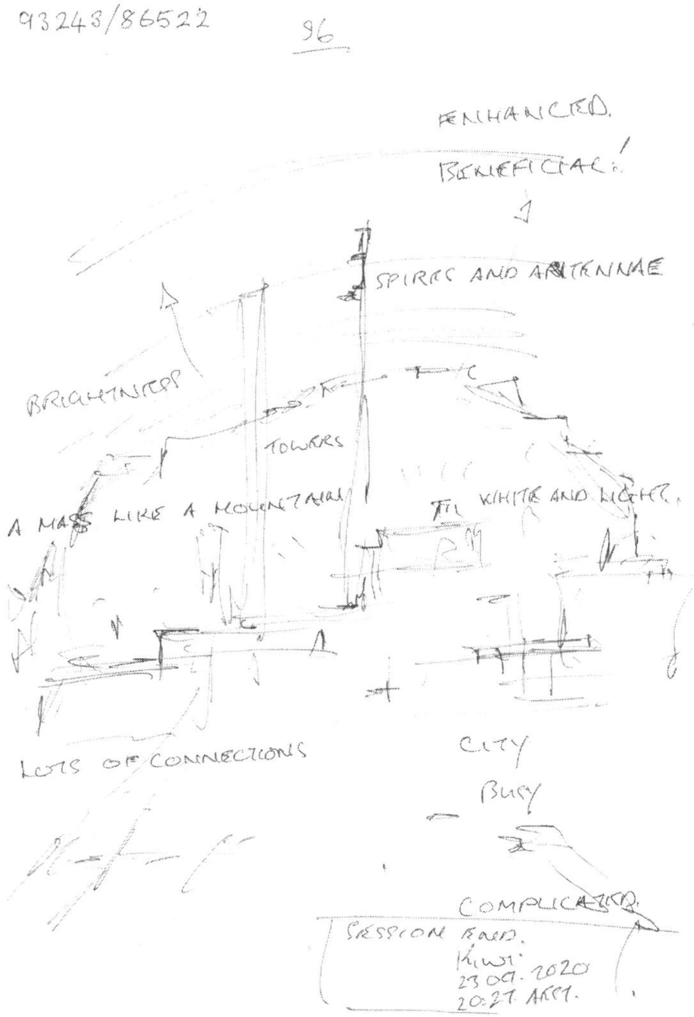
93243/86522
96
ENHANCED.
BENEFICIAL!
SPIRES AND ANTENNAE
BRIGHTNESS
TOWERS
A MASS LIKE A MOUNTAIN
WHITE AND LIGHT.
LOTS OF CONNECTIONS
CITY
BUSY
COMPLICATED.
SESSION END.
KIWI
23.09.2020
20:27 AEST.

There is ENHANCED.

There is BENEFICIAL!

There are SPIRES AND ANTENNAE.

There is BRIGHTNESS.

There are TOWERS.

Behind the structures, there is A MASS LIKE A MOUNTAIN.

There is WHITE AND LIGHT.

There are LOTS OF CONNECTIONS.

There is a CITY.

There is BUSY.

There is COMPLICATED.

Comments on the S6

Above the city and the imposing mountainous mass, there is BRIGHTNESS radiating in bands upwards and outwards. This brightness is indicated by two arrows, one on either side of the center. This emitted energy is associated with ENHANCED and BENEFICIAL!

We have BUSY as well as brightness. The large mountainous backdrop to the ancient, yet modern city, suggests challenges the project might face. The mountains also suggest the blockchain technology will enable large complex societies anywhere on the planet. Indicators of business, complexity, and LOTS OF CONNECTIONS echoes this theme.

The towers and spires also convey determination to meet the challenges. The structures radiate white light, which I interpret as a sign that this crypto project will be a notable success. The city with its towers and spires and the mountains behind it, reminded me of photos I have seen of Iranian cities.[1]

Footnote

After analyzing the data, I found an intriguing online article with a striking photo. The date of publication was only days after I had completed my remote viewing session. To my mind its relevance to the S6 could not be clearer. Now, I think it would be remiss of me if I did not mention the story in this comment section for readers to consider along with the recorded data.

It seems Iran might fully embrace cryptocurrencies soon. Clicking on the link in the endnotes of this chapter in the book will take you to an interesting photo of an Iranian city and the associated article. The title is "Iran Legalizes Use of Cryptocurrencies for Imports." I am sure you will see what I am talking about.[2]

My Conclusion for Kusama

Based on my S6 remote viewing alone, I say Kusama is a keeper.

---

1. However, during the session, I treated this idea as an intrusion by my conscious mind and labeled it an AOL, and for that reason considered it invalid data.
2. This is big news for bitcoin and cryptocurrencies in general, but I wonder, does it have anything to do with Kusama? I don't have a clear answer to that question, but I do know coincidence never explains anything. Review the story, and see if you notice the similarity between the photo at the top of the article and the S6, as I did.

   https://themarketperiodical.com/2020/10/30/iran-legalises-use-of-cryptocurrencies-for-imports/

CHAPTER 7
UNISWAP (UNI)

ABOUT UNISWAP

Price in USD: $2.85

Market Cap: $600,102,097

Circulating Supply: 210,873,266 UNI (21.09% of the total supply).

[Date and Source: 28 October, 2020; https://coinmarketcap.com/]

WP: https://uniswap.org/whitepaper.pdf

Official Website: https://uniswap.org/

Background

Uniswap is a popular trading platform. Built on the Ethereum blockchain, it has proven to be very popular; to the extent several sources, including dappradar.com and Nairametrics, rate it as the world's largest Decentralized Exchange platform, or Decentralized Finance Exchange (also known as a DEX).

Analysis

ST - Uniswap

The ST for this session follows.

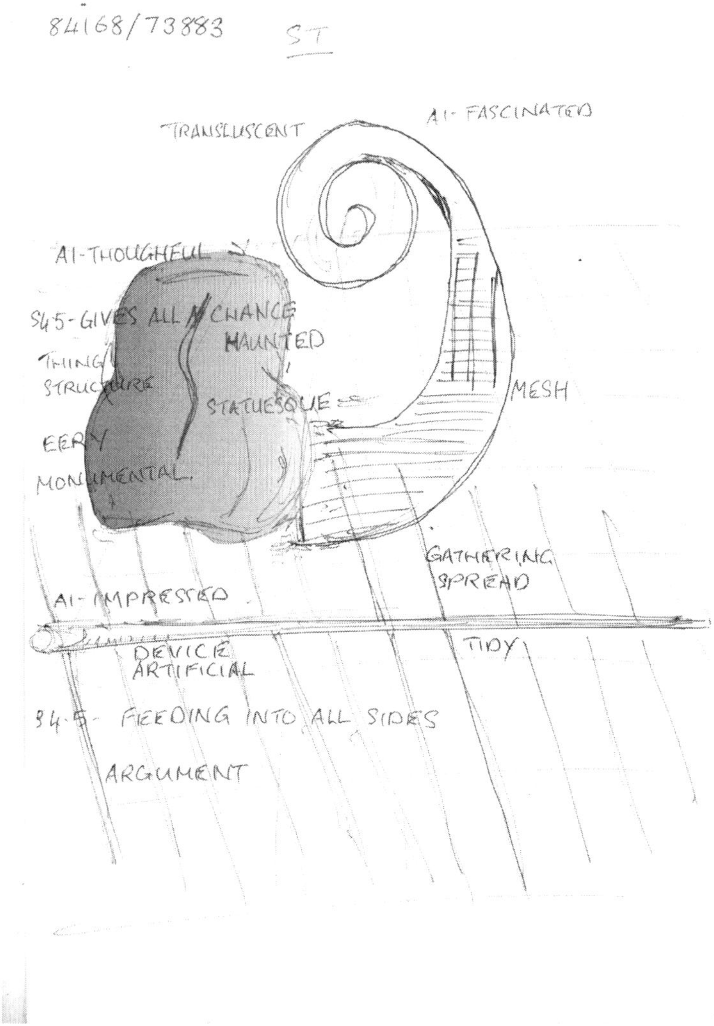
84168/73883
ST
TRANSLUSCENT
A1-FASCINATED
A1-THOUGHFUL
S4.5-GIVES ALL A CHANCE
HAUNTED
THING
STRUCTURE
STATUESQUE
MESH
EERY
MONUMENTAL
GATHERING
SPREAD
A1-IMPRESSED
DEVICE
ARTIFICIAL
TIDY
S4.5- FEEDING INTO ALL SIDES
ARGUMENT

Overview of the ST Sketch

The three aspects occupy the same site. Aspect X is the pink STRUCTURE, Aspect A is the high spiral-shaped MESH that extends from Aspect X. Aspect B is the fern or feather-like DEVICE that runs horizontally across the foreground.

X

Aspect X is a big, dense, pink, purple, and tan-colored, tall, thick, heavy THING that is a STRUCTURE. It is positioned above and on something. It has a wave-like vertical opening on the side. It is associated with HAUNTED, STATUESQUE, EERY, and MONUMENTAL.

There's the idea that it GIVES ALL A CHANCE.

It makes me feel THOUGHTFUL.

A

Aspect A is a high, upright, golden-colored glittering THING with MESH that curves in a spiral. The aspect is associated with TRANSLUCENT.

It makes me feel FASCINATED.

• • •

B

Aspect B is a light-red-and-brown-colored long, thin, tubular DEVICE that is ARTIFICIAL. It runs over, on, and across something. It is associated with GATHERING, SPREAD, TIDY, and ARGUMENT. There is the idea of FEEDING INTO ALL SIDES.

It makes me feel IMPRESSED.

S6 - The Ultimate Future of Uniswap

The final page of data from the remote viewing session follows.

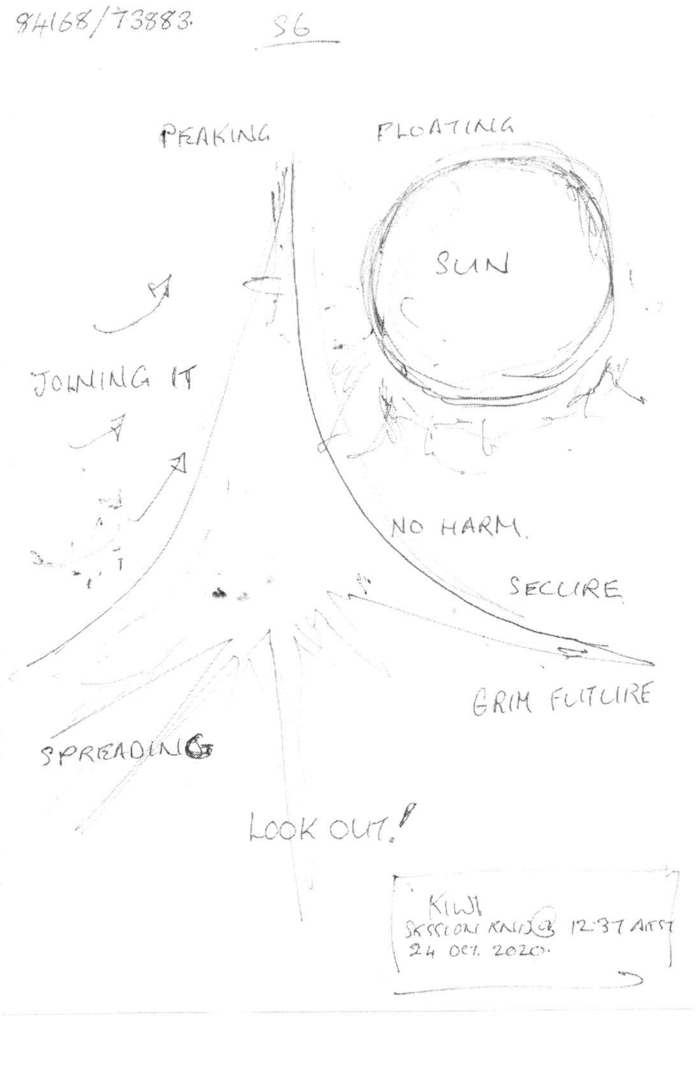
84168/73883
S6
PEAKING
FLOATING
SUN
JOINING IT
NO HARM.
SECURE
GRIM FUTURE
SPREADING
LOOK OUT!
KIWI
SESSION ENDED 12:37 AEST
24 OCT. 2020.

There is PEAKING.
There is FLOATING.
There is a SUN.
There is JOINING IT.
There is NO HARM.
There is SECURE.
There is GRIM FUTURE.
There is SPREADING.
There is LOOK OUT!

Comments on the S6

The PEAKING is significant, and many arrows show a momentum that's upwards. There is JOINING IT on one side of the peak.

A radiant SUN is FLOATING high on the right-hand side of the peak. Below the orb and beside the line that descends from the peak there is NO HARM. Further down, there is SECURE. There is a GRIM FUTURE on the end of the descending right-hand side of the line. There is also a SPREADING below the rising line toward the peak, and last there is the warning, "LOOK OUT!"

The S6 appears to indicate an early peak for this project. The arrows indicate many forces moving up toward the peak. SPREADING is linked to the warning

LOOK OUT! This alert, together with GRIM FUTURE, does not bode well for the project. Yet, the S6 data indicates there is success as well as failure. The SUN FLOATING above indicates the presence of light and life.

My Conclusion for Uniswap

The ultimate future for this crypto project is one that resists being summed up as a straight forward success or failure. Initially at least, it's heading for the moon. The stellar performance is not sustained nor repeated. Instead, it falls steadily back to Earth at a much faster rate than the gradual rate of its ascent. There can be no recovery.

I conclude that, while this is a solid project that meets most, if not all of its objectives fairly early on, its trajectory does not hold. It seems to me the crypto project will perform in a spectacular fashion, but the market will quickly become saturated and the users will dissipate.

After reviewing the remote viewing data, it looks like the best idea is to hold onto Uniswap until it looks like it is about to moon. From there, it looks to be all downhill.

Considering only my S6 data, I find Uniswap is a limited keeper.

CHAPTER 8
TRON (TRX)

ABOUT TRON

Price in USD: $0.026987

Market Cap: $1,933,906,644

Circulating Supply: 71,659,657,369 TRX (71.06% of the total supply).

[Date and Source: 28 October, 2020; https://coinmarketcap.com/]

WP: https://tron.network/static/doc/white_paper_v_2_0.pdf

Official Website: https://tron.network/

Background

When TRON first arrived on the scene, its goal was to bring change to the global entertainment industry. The team decided to focus on the growing market for Decentralized Applications (Dapps). The aim of the team being to produce a tool that serves wider human interests, rather than the profit-driven goals of a corporate elite. The goal of the project is to "cut out the middlemen" dominating the market for creators of digital content through the main digital storefront platforms. Just consider for a moment the prominent US companies that make up FANG stocks, and you'll grasp the controllers they aim to display. This crypto project appeals to me due to its courage and ambition.

Analysis

ST - Tron

The ST for this session follows.

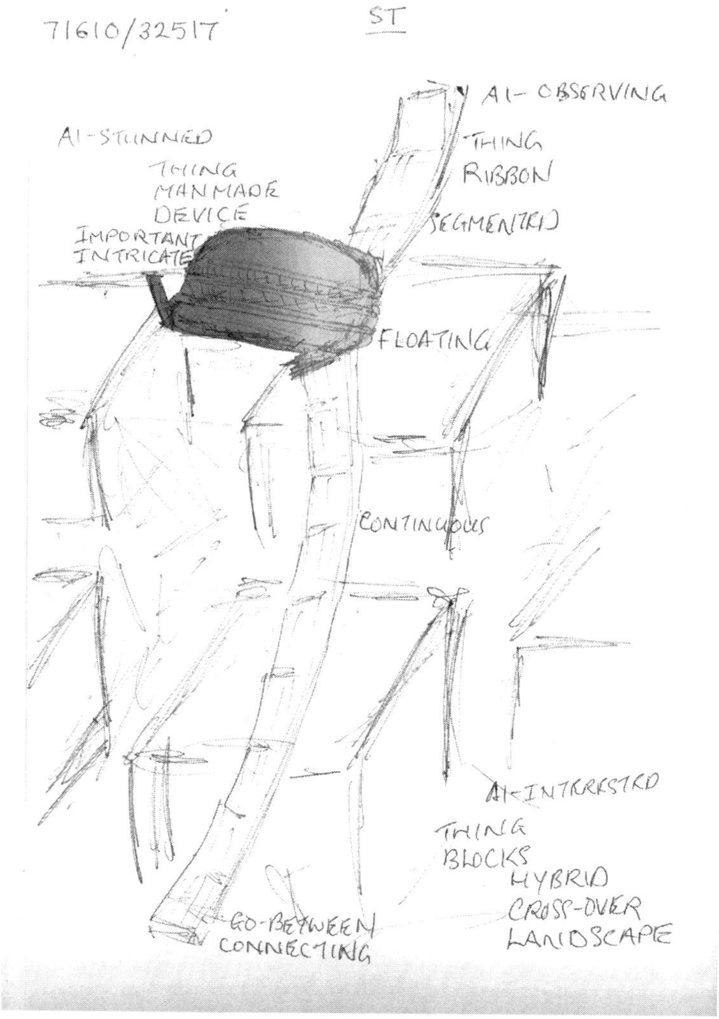
71610/32517
ST
AI- OBSERVING
THING
RIBBON
SEGMENTED
AI-STUNNED
THING
MANMADE
DEVICE
IMPORTANT
INTRICATE
FLOATING
CONTINUOUS
AI-INTERESTED
THING
BLOCKS
HYBRID
CROSS-OVER
LANDSCAPE
GO-BETWEEN
CONNECTING

Overview of the ST Sketch

These three aspects can be found at the same site. Aspect X is a MAN-MADE DEVICE that is FLOATING in the foreground. I have colored it black.

The other two aspects are directly behind Aspect X.

Aspect A is a SEGMENTED RIBBON that runs vertically down the center. Aspect B is located behind Aspect A.

Aspect B, which is made of BLOCKS, occupies a larger portion of the ST than the other two aspects.

X

The target aspect is a big, dense, curved, black-colored reflective THING. It is a MAN-MADE DEVICE positioned on a diagonal above something. It is associated with IMPORTANT, INTRICATE, and FLOATING.

The feeling it evokes in me is STUNNED.

A

Aspect A is a dark-red colored THING that's a long, thin, flat, and narrow RIBBON. It is associated with SEGMENTED, CONTINUOUS, GO-BETWEEN, and CONNECTING.

It makes me feel like OBSERVING it.

B

Aspect B is a black-colored THING made up of big, thick, dense, BLOCKS that are raised, and flat across the top and variously situated at different levels from high to low. It is associated with HYBRID, CROSS-OVER, and LANDSCAPE.

The feeling it evokes in me is INTERESTED.

S6 - The Ultimate Future of Tron

The final page of data from the remote viewing session follows.

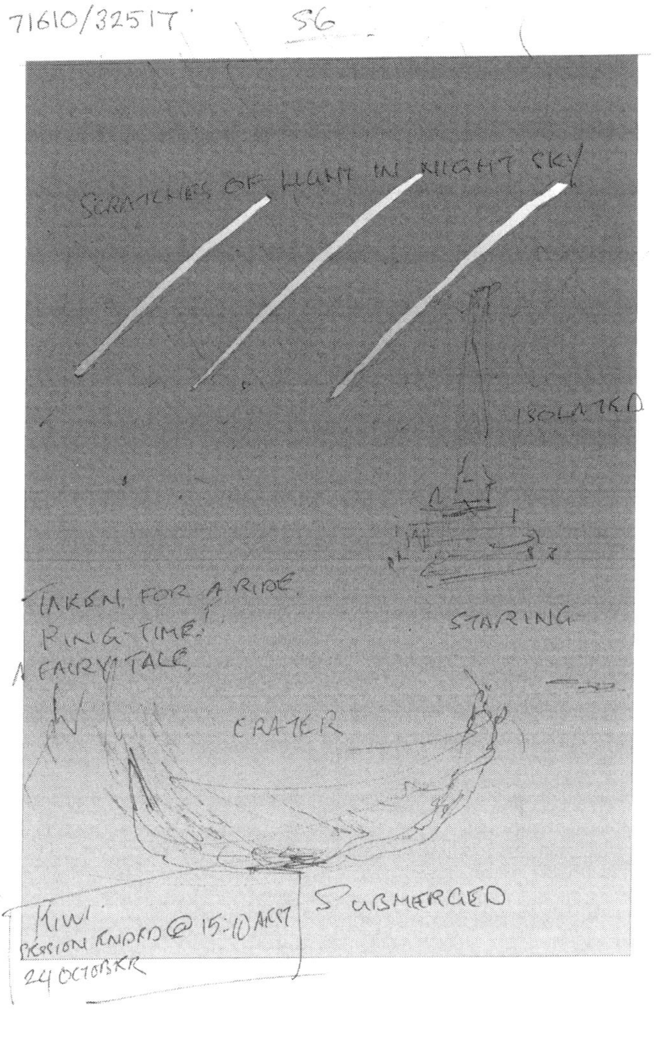
71610/32517
S6
SCRATCHES OF LIGHT IN NIGHT SKY
ISOLATED
TAKEN FOR A RIDE
RING TIME
FAIRY TALE
STARING
CRATER
SUBMERGED
KIWI
SESSION ENDED @ 15:10 AEST
24 OCTOBER

There are SCRATCHES OF LIGHT IN (the) NIGHT SKY.

There is ISOLATED.

There is TAKEN FOR A RIDE.

There is STARING.

There is RING TIME!

There is A FAIRY TALE.

There is a CRATER.

There is SUBMERGED.

Comments on the S6

The scratches resemble claw marks of a bear. The object standing alone resembles a monument. "STARING" is associated with it. The 'monument' stares into the darkness. At the base of the S6, there is a SUBMERGED CRATER.

I observe emptiness, lack of movement, and absence of brightness. I also don't see any suggestion of active lifeforms or any motion at all. Nothing is happening. The SCRATCHES OF LIGHT IN THE NIGHT SKY emphasize the surrounding darkness enveloping the S6.

ISOLATED emphasizes a sense of emptiness. Monuments inherently lack senses, which means they can't see. Therefore, STARING into the dark must be understood in a metaphorical sense. This leads me to interpret the data as metaphorical in nature. The notions of CRATER and SUBMERGED associate readily with failure. TAKEN FOR A RIDE is harshly direct, while A FAIRY TALE is gentle. These ideas indicate both deception and disappointment.

My Conclusion for Tron

Tron maintains a sizable user base and a somewhat thriving community. The data, therefore, exemplifies how remote viewing can reveal a story many might not want to hear.

Based on my S6 data alone, I have to conclude Tron is not a keeper.

CHAPTER 9
HXRO (HXRO)

ABOUT HXRO

Price in USD: $0.227494

Market Cap: $41,400,903

Circulating Supply: 181,986,452 HXRO (18.20% of the total supply).

[Date and Source: 28 October, 2020; https://coinmarketcap.com/]

WP: I can't seem to find one.

Official Website: https://www.hxro.io/

Background

A token built on the Solana blockchain, HXRO is a distributed liquidity layer that merges traditional trading with gaming to provide a fun, simple, effective, and decentralized cryptocurrency trading platform. The platform uses the terms "moon" and "rekt" to describe trader positions, with payoffs coming from the out-of-the-money traders to those in-the-money.

Analysis

ST - HXRO

The ST for this session follows.

87892/12647 ST

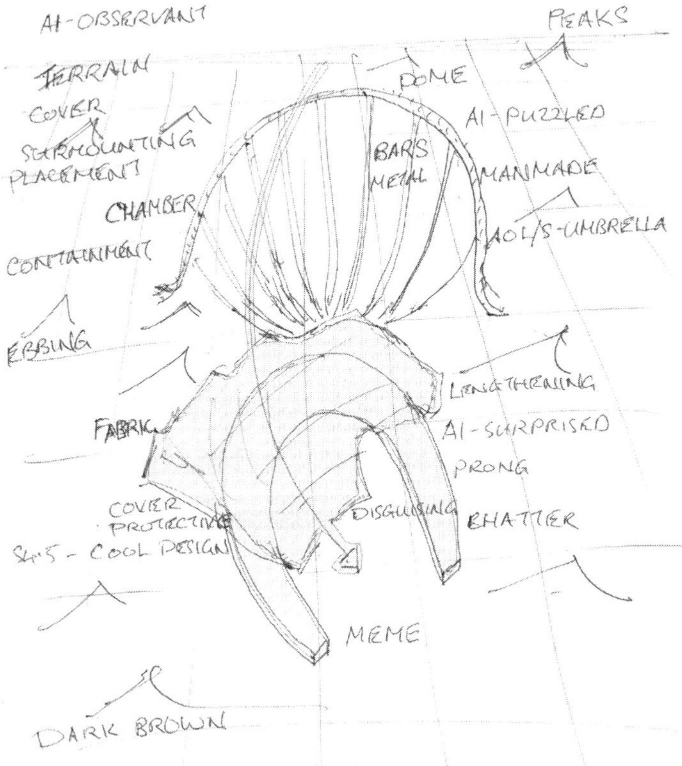

Overview of the ST Sketch

Aspect X comprises a PRONG and a FABRIC. I have colored it green. Aspect X is in the foreground. Aspect B is a DOME with METAL BARS sitting over Aspect X. A moving force, seen as a long, curving arrow in the sketch, connects both aspects. It runs over Aspect B and through Aspect X.

Aspect A represents the peak-covered TERRAIN on which Aspects X and B sit.

X

Aspect X consists of a long, thick, dense, curved, and pointed PRONG and a FABRIC positioned underneath something. There is a movement through it from north to southeast. It is associated with LENGTHENING, COVER, DISGUISING, PROTECTIVE, CHATTER, and MEME. There is the idea of a COOL DESIGN.

It makes me feel SURPRISED.

A

Aspect A consists of a wide, thick TERRAIN that has DARK BROWN colored pointed PEAKS over, on, and across it. It is associated with COVER, SURMOUNTING, PLACEMENT, CONTAINMENT, and EBBING.

It makes me feel OBSERVANT.

B

There is a strongly recurring idea of UMBRELLA.

Aspect B is MAN-MADE and consists of a dark, shiny, illuminated DOME with METAL BARS that is positioned above and over something. It is associated with CHAMBER.

It makes me feel PUZZLED.

S6 - The Ultimate Future of Hxro

The final page of data from the remote viewing session is provided below.

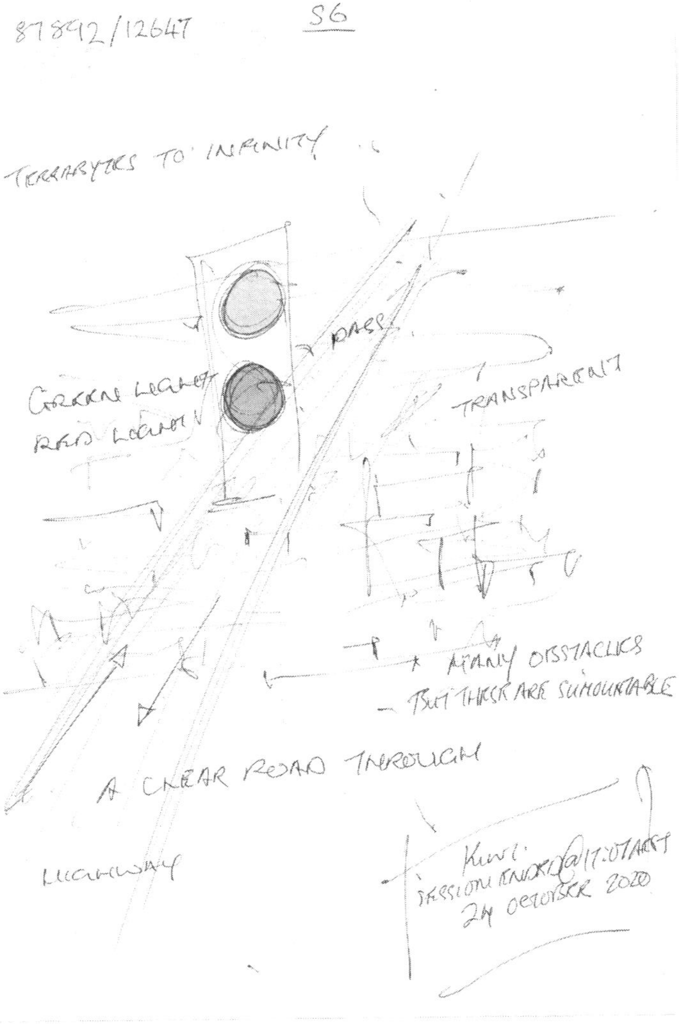
87892/12647
S6
TERRABYTES TO INFINITY
PASS
GREEN LIGHT
RED LIGHT
TRANSPARENT
MANY OBSTACLES
BUT THESE ARE SURMOUNTABLE
A CLEAR ROAD THROUGH
HIGHWAY
KIWI
SESSION ENDED @ 17:07 AEST
24 OCTOBER 2020

There are TERABYTES TO INFINITY.

There is PASS.

There is a GREEN LIGHT and a RED LIGHT.

There is TRANSPARENT.

There are MANY OBSTACLES. BUT THESE ARE SURMOUNTABLE.

There is a CLEAR ROAD THROUGH.

There is HIGHWAY.

Comments on the S6

There's a HIGHWAY running similarly to A CLEAR ROAD THROUGH something. It stretches from the bottom to the top. Traffic on the left moves upwards, while on the right, it goes in the opposite direction.

There is a set of vertically positioned traffic lights either on or above the road. The GREEN LIGHT is above the RED LIGHT. On the road above the lights, there is PASS. Below the highway or road and on both sides there are blocky structures, which appear to have a TRANSPARENT quality.

There are difficulties, but these are not impossible to overcome.

My Conclusion for Hxro

HXRO manages vast amounts of data, indicating robust performance. The data reveals the project is a showcase of potential and transparency. There is organization and a means of control. Overall, it looks to be well-engineered, and able to deal with the various problems it will encounter.

These are pleasing indicators. There is nothing apparent in the S6 data suggesting to me future problems of the kind that will do serious damage to the cryptocurrency project. It is solid enough to be assessed as successful by who would appraise it.

Based only on the S6 data, I conclude that the token is promising and worth holding onto. HXRO is a keeper!

CHAPTER 10
CONCLUSIONS

- **Chainlink (LINK)** - Success.
- **Hxro (HXRO)** - Success.
- **Kusama (KSM)** - Success.
- **Tron (TRX)** - Fail.
- **Uniswap (UNI)** - Success. But, watch out! It looks like it eventually falls suddenly after a peak!
- **Velas (VLX)** - Fail.

Thank you for your purchase!

PLEASE SCAN *the QR code to leave a review or star rating.*

I'm excited to share the insights from my remote viewing explorations. As a reader, your perspective is invaluable—not just to me, but to other readers also. Feedback helps books like mine find their audience. So, please take a minute or two to post an honest review or a quick rating.

If this was your introduction to the vast world of remote viewing and cryptocurrency, congratulations! You have reached the end of Book One. I hope you found my remote viewing of some value to you, even if only to help narrow down the coins you think you might want to learn more about.

Warmly,

Kiwi Joe

ABOUT THE AUTHOR

I started my Technical Remote Viewing (TRV) training in early 2010. TRV was developed by Major Ed Dames (US Army Retired). It is the next iteration of the original CRV protocol taught in the US Army to hand-picked recruits. There are several mainstream branches that stem from CRV, each with its unique flavor. They adhere to a similar step-by-step structure, a discipline distinguishing remote viewers from psychics.

If you're keen on mastering this skill, I recommend finding a teacher. Don't delay. The rewards of practicing remote viewing are significant. This is a journey of discovery that will forever change your perception of the world and yourself.

Apart from remote viewing, I lead a typical life with my family. I hope you enjoyed the book. Be safe out there, and keep your eyes open to the possibilities.

If you have a question or suggestion you think I can

respond to, please feel free to email me. I read all the correspondence I get from readers and do my best to answer promptly.

kiwijoe.rv@gmail.com

You can also find me here:

https://www.facebook.com/KiwiJoesRemoteViewing/

https://www.bookbub.com/profile/kiwi-joe

ALSO BY KIWI JOE

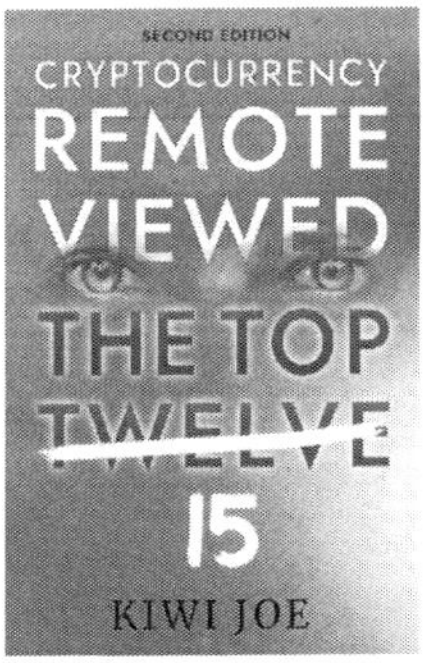

The 'Cryptocurrency Remote Viewed' series covers sixty-six cryptos. They are Kiwi Joe's top twelve picks from those he has covered so far. They include an additional bonus coin, and because this is the 2nd edition, another three cryptos! You will be surprised at the bargains available in this volatile market. These coins and tokens are deemed worthy of HODLing based solely on Joe's analysis of the remote viewing data.

Book Seven is packed full of background and remote viewing data, guiding readers on what to search for in more conventional information sources. This book targets seasoned remote viewers, cryptocurrency enthusiasts, and those seeking a research edge in crypto projects.

The book delves into twelve coins and tokens, each chapter detailing its background and its future as revealed by my remote viewing. The remote viewing information offers insights into crypto projects that traditional sources might overlook. Each chapter concludes with a definitive statement on the cryptocurrency's long-term viability based on remote viewing results.

The cryptocurrencies covered in this book are as follows:

- **Ankr (ANKR)**
- **Dash (DASH)**
- **Decred (DCR)**
- **Fantom (FTM)**
- **GateToken (GT)**
- **Handshake (HNS)**
- **Hive (HIVE)**
- **Maker (MKR)**

- **SingularityNET (AGIX)**
- **Terra (LUNA)**
- **Unibright (UBT)**
- **Wanchain (WAN)**

Book Six further expands the series. Kiwi Joe provides a deeper background of each project than in the previous books, includes an extended analysis of the remote viewing data and introduces new sections for added clarity and detail. The coins covered are the following:

- **Ark (ARK)**
- **Binance Coin (BNB)**
- **Bitcoin Gold (BTG)**
- **Bitshares (BTS)**
- **EOS (EOS)**
- **Mysterium (MYST)**
- **OXEN (OXEN)**
- **Reserve Rights (RSR)**
- **SERUM (SRM)**
- **STORJ (STORJ)**
- **SushiSwap (SUSHI)**
- **TomoChain (TOMO)**

Book Five evaluates the performance of the targeted cryptos and covers ten remote viewing sessions. He tells you which of the coins below are the long-term winners and which are the losers.

- **Celo (CELO)**
- **Gnosis (GNO)**
- **Loopring (LRC)**
- **MonaCoin (MONA)**
- **Monero (XMR)**
- **NEAR Protocol (NEAR)**
- **Numeraire (NMR)**
- **RedFOX Labs (RFOX)**
- **Streamr (DATA)**
- **SwissBorg (CHSB)**

Remote viewing focuses solely on the truth. All the cryptos covered in the series are taken from a blind target pool compiled from the top 190 as ranked according to market cap in late October 2020. The use of a blind pool is the standard approach remote viewers take to avoid corrupting their session by having foreknowledge of the target.

In Book Four the remote viewing sessions reveals the winners and losers among the following coins:

- **Ardor (ARDR)**
- **Basic Attention Token (BAT)**
- **Cronos (CRO)**
- **Nano (NANO)**
- **Orchid (OXT)**
- **Theta Fuel (TFUEL)**
- **Thunder Token (TT)**
- **TitanSwap (TITAN)**
- **XRP (XRP)**
- **Zilliqa (ZIL)**

Book Three offers a chapter guiding newcomers on how to analyze remote viewing data.

The book reveals the winners and losers according to the remote viewing data among the following coins:

- **Adex Network (ADX)**
- **Aeternity (AE)**
- **RSK Infrastructure Framework (RIF)**
- **Solana (SOL)**
- **Synthetix (SNX)**
- **Switcheo (SWTH)**
- **Xinfin Network (XDC)**
- **Neo (NEO)**

Book Two showcases some essential remote viewing sessions with Kiwi Joe targeting eight cryptos, one of which is Bitcoin. In addition, in the 'How We Do This' chapter, the book demonstrates aspects of remote viewing analysis in more detail using the crypto project Horizen as an example. The following coins and tokens are covered in the book:

- **Augur (REP)**
- **Bitcoin (BTC)**
- **Gxchain (GXC)**
- **Horizen (ZEN)**
- **Mimblewimblecoin (MWC)**
- **Mx Token (MX)**
- **Steem (STEEM)**
- **Yearn.Finance (YFI)**

Cryptos are soaring, but there are surprises to come. Some will be not so good, and some will be very good. This series uses remote viewing to predict the ultimate future for various cryptos. It shows you the winners and the losers, and for the latter, it's those crypto-assets you should take a good hard look at before you leap in. Only remote viewing gives you this kind of pre-warning.

"Cryptocurrency Remote Viewed Book One" is available for FREE download (i.e., the ebook).

Discover what the future has in store for the following cryptos:

- **Chainlink (LINK)**
- **Hxro (HXRO)**
- **Kusama (KSM)**
- **Tron (TRX)**
- **Uniswap (UNI)**
- **Velas (VLX)**

This is the 2nd Edition of 'Most Secret Weapons of Nations Remote Viewed'—Book IV in the Remote Viewed series. Guaranteed to fascinate and disturb you, in turn. All the targets explored were drawn from a blind pool used by Kiwi Joe in practice sessions over a period of six years. They comprise eighteen sessions covering ten countries. Nine of the ten weapons remain secret with two of them hidden in plain sight.

As you might expect from a book on the subject, it contains some startling and troubling information. One of its conclusions is that the entire globe is now a battlefield. The original sketches from the remote viewing sessions illustrate the book. Read it now, if you dare.

The question of how we address the continuing radioactive seep from the disabled Nuclear Power Plant has been remote viewed and the answer found. The bad news is that the sheer scale of the project presents a real challenge to engineers. The good news is that it can be done, so long as there exists the will to do it. The problem of scale did not deter the ancients from building the pyramids of Giza. So, we know stopping the radiation leak at the Daiichi Power Plant can be done.

Ironically, in light of the above, Japan is considering a proposal to build the gigantic Shimizu Mega-City Pyramid over Tokyo Bay. The concept was first made public just three years after the Fukushima Daiichi melt-downs, which seems to raise a question of priorities. The economic welfare of a nation is critical to its population's health, but isn't the health of the nation also reliant on the well-being of its people?

In 2012, Kiwi Joe was a member of a remote viewing team blind tasked to find the best solution. While the work done by the rest of the team can't be included in this book, the vast majority of that data lines up with what he gathered in his remote viewing sessions. This book outlines the necessary steps and offers observations based on analysis of the remote viewing data.

The book is illustrated with drawings from two remote viewing sessions completed while Kiwi Joe was part of the team. It includes the final session, which resembles a blueprint. It shows the three main steps needed. Along with endnotes citing the sources used in writing the background for this book, there is a resource list for those who want more information about remote viewing. The author includes his contact details in the back if readers have questions or suggestions for him.

Important update: Forrest Fenn confirmed the treasure chest's discovery to the Santa Fe New Mexican on June 07, 2020. Congratulations to the finder!

This book marks the second installment in the Remote Viewed series. It covers many remote viewing sessions that targeted the location of Forrest Fenn's treasure chest. The book aimed to help readers verify solutions and strategies, rethink them where necessary, and pose critical questions they may not otherwise have considered.

Kiwi Joe explains the meaning of two of the most important clues in Forrest Fenn's poem, and shows the location of the chest within a one-and-a-half-mile radius. He also provides a bird's-eye view and perspectives from higher altitudes. Finally, he shows how the data points to the specific region in the Rocky Mountains.

There are 21 illustrations in total taken from six extended remote view sessions. Additionally, there's a resource list including literature and online sources. There is something for both treasure hunters and remote viewers alike.

Important update: Forrest Fenn confirmed the treasure chest's discovery to the Santa Fe New Mexican on June 07, 2020. Congratulations to the finder!

Kiwi Joe was on the lookout for a suitable popular mystery to demonstrate the power of remote viewing. Mr. Fenn's treasure hunt was perfect for the project, and with the agreement of his client, he released two books using the session work he had completed for himself. The detailed remote viewing maps and accompanying data are significant for treasure hunters.

This first book alone offered significant information to decode Forrest Fenn's cryptic clues, verify solutions and strategies, and prompt rethinking where necessary. The book reveals how Mr. Fenn positioned the chest so that a treasure hunter close to the site could throw a rock at it.

There is a bird's eye view of the immediate area, and as a bonus, Kiwi Joe gives the reader a peek inside the chest.

The book includes 16 full-page illustrations from five remote view sessions and the analysis of the data with conclusions. Additionally, there's a resource list of relevant literature as well as other online sources for both treasure hunters and remote viewers. The book is divided into two parts, with all illustrations in the second part.

BIBLIOGRAPHY

NB: The list is far from comprehensive, but it does give an idea of the range of publications on the subject of Remote Viewing.

Remote Viewing

Brown, C. (2005). *Remote Viewing: The Science and Theory of Nonphysical Perception.*

Buchanan, L. (2003). *The Seventh Sense: The Secrets of Remote Viewing as Told by a "Psychic Spy" for the US Military.*

Dames, E. (2010). *Tell Me What You See: Remote Viewing Cases from the World's Premier Psychic Spy.*

Knowles, J. (2017). *Remote Viewing from the Ground Up.*

William, L. L. (2017). *Monitoring: A Guide for Remote Viewing & Professional Intuitive Teams.*

Marrs, J. (2007). *PSI Spies: The True Story of America's Psychic Warfare Program.*

McMoneagle, J. (2000). *Remote Viewing Secrets: A Handbook for extending and developing your psychic abilities.*

Morehouse, D. (1998). *Psychic Warrior: Inside the CIA's Stargate Program: The True Story of a Soldier's Espionage and Awakening.*

Noble, J., & Coronado, Pam. (2018). *Natural Remote Viewing: A practical guide to the mental martial art of self-discovery.*

Puthoff, H. E. (2002). Searching for the Universal Matrix in

Metaphysics. *Research New and Opportunities and Theology,* 2(8).

Rifat, T. (2003). *Remote Viewing: What it is, Who Uses it and How to do it*

Ronson, J. (2005). *The Men Who Stare at Goats.*

Schwartz, S. A. (1976). *The Secret Vaults of Time: Psychic Archaeology and the Quest for Man's Beginnings.*

Smith, D. (2013). *CRV - Controlled Remote Viewing: Manuals, collected papers & information to help you learn Controlled Remote Viewing.*

Smith, D. (2015). *Remote Viewing Dialogues: Psychic Spy Veterans from the 23 Year, US Military and Intelligence Remote Viewing Programs, Share their Expertise.*

Smith, P. (2005). *Reading the Enemy's Mind: Inside Star Gate: America's Psychic Espionage Program.*

Smith, P. H., & Feather, Sally Rhine. (2015). *The Essential Guide to Remote Viewing: The Secret Military Remote Perception Skill Anyone Can Learn.*

Stuart, B. (2016). *Technical Remote Viewing: The Complete Guide.*

Swann, I. (2018). *Everybody's Guide to Natural ESP.*

Swann, I. (2018). *Penetration: The Question of Extraterrestrial and Human Telepathy.*

Targ, R. (2004). *Limitless Mind: A Guide to Remote Viewing and Transformation of Consciousness.*

Targ, R. (2012). *The Reality of ESP: A Physicists's Proof of Psychic Abilities.*

Thompson Smith, A. (2019). *Tactical Remote Viewing.*

Vivanco, J. (2016). *The Time Before the Secret Words: On the path of remote viewing, high strangeness and zen.*

Made in the USA
Monee, IL
29 October 2025

33198352R00063